This edition of
Uniforms of Napoleon's Army
first published 2002 by Greenhill Books, Lionel Leventhal Limited, Park House, 1 Russell Gardens, London NW11 9NN
and
Stackpole Books, 5067 Ritter Road, Mechanicsburg, PA 17055, USA

© Musée de l'Armée, 2001
English-language text © Lionel Leventhal Limited, 2002

Designed by Alessandra Scarpa
Translated by Jonathan North

British Library Cataloguing in Publication Data
Vernet, Carle
Uniforms of Napoleon's army
1. France. Armee - Uniforms 2. France - History - Consulate and First Empire, 1799–1815
I. Title
355.1'4'0944'09034

ISBN 1-85367-520-2

Library of Congress Cataloging-in-Publication Data available

Publishing History
Uniforms of Napoleon's Army is an
English-language edition of
Uniformes Napoléoniens, published
by the Musée de l'Armée and
Bibliothèque de l'Image in 2001.

CARLE VERNET

UNIFORMS OF NAPOLEON'S ARMY

Greenhill Books, London
Stackpole Books, Pennsylvania

CARLE VERNET AND THE UNIFORM REGULATIONS OF THE IMPERIAL ARMY OF 1812

The manuscript of the uniform regulations of 1812 is one of the French Ministry of Defence's most treasured items. Although it is well known amongst specialists, the general public has been largely unaware of this material and of the beautiful plates now presented in this edition.

UNIFORM REGULATIONS BEFORE 1812

According to Major Bardin, who sat on the committee charged with drawing up new uniform regulations in 1811, the question of how the French Army should be clothed had always been subject to uncertainties. Even if some steps had been taken – especially during the reign of Louis XIV – to harmonise the uniforms of the different branches of service, no all-embracing regulation had ever been forthcoming.

The watercolours, gouaches and prints in the so-called Delaistre albums, named after the artist who seems to have been the principal author of the work, give the state of dress – it would be wrong, at this stage, to call them uniforms – of the troops serving in the king's armies in the years around the time of the end of the Regency and the return of the young Louis XV to Versailles (1721–1722). The albums, which were undertaken as part of the young king's military education, might have suggested a vision of how the royal army should have appeared, as well as indicating how weapons should have been carried or drill performed, but they are not linked to any specific change in the practices of the time. Nevertheless, they seem to suggest that the standardisation of military dress was, in theory if not in practice, on the advance.

In the eighteenth century a number of ordinances and regulations were issued in an attempt to instil some order in uniform practices that were, for the most part, left to the whim of a commanding officer. A few collections of prints or drawings, mostly from the second half of the century, and mostly illustrating particular branches of service, supply us with some details of how troops in particular regiments were dressed.

The regulation issued in 1786, the most complete to date, was not supported by any print or drawing which might have thrown some light on which practices were continued and which were newly introduced. It would serve, almost without change, the armies of the Revolution, the Directory, the Consulate and even the imperial regime, much to the indignation of Bardin. He thought it insufficient and inappropriate for an army linked indelibly to revolution:

'These regulations pander to the whims of colonels who, capricious and powerful, choose colours most pleasing to their own eye. Innovations or modifications were brought or solicited as favours or conceits and were invoked because such and such a mistress adored light blue; or because another had a fondness for yellow or another had a passion for crimson; or even because a colonel wanted nothing more than to dress his soldiers in the livery of his lover. It would have been a wise thing to do to put an end to these perpetual variations and to end the plague of duels which were frequently caused by sarcastic comments about uniforms. Who can count how many duels stemmed from the fact that the Régiment du Roi had adopted twenty-four buttons on its coat and the Régiment de Navarre twenty-five? It can be seen that such convulsions in colour were a matter of deep intrigue in the offices of Versailles or in ministerial bureaux.'

Year VIII (1800) witnessed, for the first time since 1792, the return of a more ordered code of dress, one harmonised if not yet systematic, but it again went unaccompanied by any visual guide. The regulations were prone to certain variations when actually applied and, as Bardin lamented, 'military costume can no longer be termed military costume as it is subject to caprice and frivolity, and to the vagaries of fashion'.

Only during the height of empire would a project be implemented to properly regulate the dress and equipment of French soldiers. The Imperial Guard had, since the early days of the regime, shown some of the most outrageous examples of variation in dress, an example quickly followed by the rest of the Army. Such methods wrought havoc in the manufacture of clothing and brought financial confusion.

THE BOURCIER COMMISSION

In July 1811, in an attempt to clear up the confusion, Napoleon set up a commission to establish the uniform of the French Army. Bourcier, a councillor of state, presided over the working group which included General Sorbier, representing the artillery; Colonel Dauttencourt, for the cavalry; Major Bardin, for the infantry; and Intendant Dufour for the administrative staff. It was given the task of 'defining the dimension and cut of each item of clothing'.

Major Bardin recounted, in 1818, how the committee set about its given task. The committee assembled at the Depot de la Guerre and would begin by laying down the principles of how each individual item of dress should be produced as well as commenting on those items of equipment not yet regulated. The draft findings would then be sent to the Ministry of War for approval and, following such, would be issued as regulations.

Bardin, who, according to his own account, wanted to go further, suggested that the committee profit from the occasion and instigate a more far-reaching reform of military dress for the imperial troops. He thought that such regulations should be supported by detailed descriptions and drawings of how the troops should appear. The 1786 regulations could then be, once and for all, superseded by a definitive document, one that was simple and long lasting. Bardin also suggested that the Imperial Guard, a body always jealous of its privileges, be subject to a similar treatment.

The committee agreed with Bardin on his initial suggestion and charged him with carrying out his proposal. Colonel Dauttencourt was, however, given the task of working on issues connected to equipment. Bardin began work but the commission,

'. . . Refused to include the Imperial Guard as this unit – or rather this army – always proved troublesome. The commission avoided getting entangled and was not motivated out of patriotism but, rather, wished to avoid ruffling the Guard's eminent leadership. These influential men, rich and powerful, immediately rendered any attempt at revision too delicate a subject.'

The task was immense but was accomplished with such astonishing speed and vigour that any attempt to hinder or obstruct it largely failed.

The draft drawings were done by artists working in the Depot for a fee of 15,000 francs whilst Carle Vernet, a famous artist, was given the task of painting miniatures – one-tenth the actual size – of 'an officer and soldier of each of the Army's line units'. He would be paid 16,000 francs.

Each item of uniform was drawn twice in full-size or half-size. One copy was engraved and issued as an accompaniment to the text, having been annotated with all the necessary dimensions for the manufacture of each item. The other was coloured in order to be presented to the emperor for approval.

The text was also drafted in two versions – one to present to the emperor, the other, an incredibly detailed document, was intended to form the published regulation.

The text was published in early 1812. On 19 January an imperial decree 'Regarding the Uniform of Foot Soldiers' was issued, followed, on 7 February, by one 'Regarding the Uniform of Mounted Troops'. These appeared in the *Journal Militaire* as well as in Goupil's *Manual for the administration and issue of clothing* (published by Magimel) and Berriat's work on military law.

A decree issued on 12 April 1812 stipulated however that the replacement of existing items could only take place in 1813. The new uniform was, on the whole, more expensive than the one it was replacing. It is therefore difficult to evaluate to what extent the new uniform was adopted despite the fact that the emperor had hoped to have it before his departure for Russia.

The uniform was put into service in 1813. However, a large part of the Army was in Spain while much of the rest was reorganising in Germany. It is therefore probable that, given the circumstances, other priorities negated the importance of the uniform regulations.

THE PLATES

The complete collection comprising the 'Regulation on dress, apparel, distinctive marks, equipment and armament of the troops of the French Army, as well as the harnessing of the cavalry and officers' horses' is preserved in the library of the Musée de l'Armée in Paris. There the four volumes destined for the Minister of War and the emperor can be found – loaned from the Service Historique de l'Armée de Terre since 1978 – along with Bardin's working manuscript, which was donated by Widow Millot in 1901. The official collection is made up of the following volumes:

Volume One

The manuscript of the regulation's text. Divided into four parts it deals with the following:

– the overall intention of the regulations for all branches of service: infantry, artillery and support troops; carabiniers, cuirassiers, dragoons, light cavalry and support troops.

– the infantry: foot gendarmes, line infantry, artillery, engineers and foreign troops; light infantry and auxiliary troops.

– the cavalry: mounted gendarmes, carabiniers, cuirassiers, dragoons, artillery train, engineers and military equipage units; light cavalry (gendarmes, lancers, hussars, chasseurs and light-horse), horse artillery.

– the staff, officers without appointment, administrative and medical staff: marshals of the empire, generals, staff officers attached to armies and garrisons, engineer officers; revenue inspectors, commissary officers, medical officers attached to hospitals and armies, and administrative staff of hospitals.

This text was not intended for publication rather, according to a note by Bardin, it was designed for presentation to the Minister of War and the emperor. Bardin also added that the volume included more regulations than were actually issued.

Volume Two

Detailed working drawings, annotated and numbered, to accompany the text showing, to scale or slightly reduced, all the different elements of dress, badges of rank, marks of distinction, equipment, harnessing and armament. The drawings were to be engraved and issued along with the text of the regulations.

Volume Three

Draft drawings, unmarked and unnumbered, accompanied by watercolour and gouache plates intended for presentation to the emperor.

Volume Four

The illustrations of Carle Vernet representing, on foot, the officers and soldiers of all the different branches of service in their different uniforms – full dress, full dress service, society dress, campaign dress – all scaled at one-tenth actual size.

The volumes were presented in a sumptuous binding of green morocco leather, with gilded iron, and with the imperial coat of arms on the frontispiece. The last volume has a simpler covering, only its back cover resembles the others.

It is material from the fourth volume which is reproduced here – seventy-six of the 244 plates. In addition to the volumes listed above there are two further volumes of text. It was this text that was destined for publication and distribution as regulations; the proofs bear corrections and annotations in the hand of Major Bardin. These marks consist of final corrections brought about by the commission or by the emperor himself.

CARLE VERNET

Antoine-Charles-Horace Vernet, known as Carle Vernet, was the third son of Joseph Vernet – a painter of landscapes and maritime subjects – and his British wife, Virginia Parker.

He grew up surrounded by the heady atmosphere of the Parisian art world in which his father occupied a most prominent place. Young Vernet would develop into an artist of note in his own right, a man of the world with a fondness for horses and Parisian fashions.

He was gifted with a precocious talent and, under his father's guidance, developed an eye for drawing. When he was eleven years old, his father entrusted him to his colleague Leipicié who undertook to teach him the art of painting.

From an early age, he had a passion for horses and for riding, a passion that stayed with him throughout his career. He was among the first French painters to frequent circuses, arenas and stables to observe horses in every situation. He was himself a talented rider and took part in sporting events or rode until he was quite advanced in years.

He entered the French Academy's prestigious Prix de Rome in 1779, coming second, and then again in 1782. In that year he was awarded first prize for his painting *The Parable of the Prodigal Son*. He then set out for Rome to undertake the mandatory period of study. He studied the works of Salvator Roas, Rafael and Jules Romain. Whilst in Rome he seems to have undergone a kind of emotional crisis, one that aroused a desire to take holy orders. Vernet's father, hearing of this through the director of the Academy, recalled his son to Paris after just six months. The crisis passed and Vernet took to painting with a passion. He began *The Triumph of Paul-Emile*, a subject that allowed him to give free rein to his love for horses and military panoply. He worked on the painting for five years before having it exhibited in 1789 at the Royal Academy of Painting and Sculpture.

Carle Vernet was profoundly affected by the revolution. His sister Emilie, married to the architect Chalgrin, who was himself an *émigré,* was found guilty by a revolutionary tribunal and executed in 1794. Vernet had entreated his colleague David to intervene but the latter declined to do so, leading to a falling-out between the two men – something which could have damaged Vernet's career.

The Directory period saw a reawakening of a more frivolous climate, one in which Vernet worked on various studies of horses, engraved by Debucourt, as well as his famous series entitled *Incredible and Marvellous.* He also worked on a series of drawings illustrating Parisian costume and these were published by Le Mésangère from 1797.

Vernet chose to accompany the First Consul, Bonaparte, on his Second Italian Campaign. His drawings, engraved by Duplessi-Bertaux, were issued from 1799 under the title *Historical Scenes of the Italian Campaigns* and they covered events from the battle of Millesimo on 14 April 1796 to Marengo on 14 June 1800.

Around this time Vernet, whilst he was working on a scene from the battle of Marengo, undertook some work for the Depot de la Guerre. Vernet was commissioned to produce a frontispiece for the account of Marengo, rewritten by Marshal Berthier according to Napoleon's instructions, for publication in 1805. The year after that he contributed a frontispiece to the account of Austerlitz and worked on various designs of Berthier's coat of arms for his official seals and stamps.

Vernet however never abandoned his love for grand historical painting. He exhibited his sketches for his study of Marengo at the Salon of 1806, although the work itself would not be finished for another four years, then followed, in 1808, his *Morning of Austerlitz,* an equestrian portrait of the emperor, the *Bombardment of Madrid* and the *Battle of Rivoli,* the latter intended for Berthier's private gallery in the Grosbois chateau. Then Vernet was selected to illustrate the Bourcier Commission's findings in 1811–1812.

In 1814 Vernet continued to work for the Bourbons, one of the few painters to successfully do so. He worked on some royal portraits, such as an equestrian painting of the Duke of Berry, as well as on some hunting and racing scenes. He also undertook some grander projects, such as the *Taking of Pamplona* in 1824. Meanwhile he continued to produce fine representations of Parisian life, including the *Costume Collection,* engraved by Debucourt and issued from 1814; the *Cries of Paris,* lithographed by Delpech around 1820; *Various Scenes and Costumes,* lithographed by Adam in 1831; *Horses of all Types,* engraved by Levachez; and *Horses from Every Country,* lithographed by Lasteyrie. He also continued to produce some uniform studies, collaborating with his son Horace on *Uniforms of the French Armies, 1791–1814,* lithographed by Delpech and *French Uniforms from 1814 to 1824,* lithographed by Villain in 1825.

He continued to work for the Depot de la Guerre but was denied his honorific grant of 1,000 francs when the military administration was forced to economise. However, he was retained to work according to requirements, budgets allowing.

In 1829 Vernet journeyed to Rome to join his son Horace, now director of the French Academy in that city. He returned in 1833 and continued to paint and to ride horses until he died, in Paris, in 1835.

VERNET'S ILLUSTRATIONS FOR THE 1812 REGULATIONS

The 244 gouaches produced by Vernet and his assistants were presented along the lines of an order of battle. Marshals of the empire, generals, the regiments of the Guard of Paris – which the regulations would actually abolish, line infantry, light infantry, the Swiss regiments, the veterans, the mounted gendarmes, the carabiniers, the cuirassiers, the dragoons, the cavalry's veterinary surgeons, the mounted chasseurs, the hussars, the light-horse lancers – including the Poles, the artillery, the horse artillery, the engineers and the topographical engineers all followed on, one after the other.

Bardin, our only source for the exact instructions passed on to Vernet, states that the artist was charged with representing 'an officer and soldier from each branch of the regular army'. The surviving plates do not, however, illustrate all the regiments or all the various ranks. According to Bardin some of the plates had already disappeared by 1818 whilst others, it seems, had succumbed to less than delicate handling. The majority of this important body of work has, however, survived intact.

Each plate is square and finished in a mixture of watercolour and gouaches. The images are enclosed in a border that is supposed to set the figures off with a *trompe d'oeil* effect. The lower part of the border originally comprised an elaborate scroll upon which a descriptive legend was to be inscribed. Not all such legends were completed, however. The text gave the branch of service, the name or number of the unit, the rank of the figures illustrated and the chief features of the uniform represented.

It should be noted that the drawings should have represented all ranks and grades of officer along with all kinds of different uniform for different occasions. These would include full dress, undress, working dress, and cloaks. Society dress, for the officers, not mentioned in the regulations, was also presented.

It is possible to distinguish a number of hands behind the creation of the plates. Vernet's work, of course, stands out on account of its quality and style; his mastery of space and positioning, his command of anatomy, the confidence of his drawing and the excellence of his colouring are all perceptible. Vernet reserved his best talent for the horses – a subject close to his heart – and these stand out and rank among the very best examples of his painting.

The figures represented in many ways resemble the work he undertook for La Mésangère in the period around 1810 – *Parisian Costumes.* This body of work also included a few examples of military uniform.

The contrast between Vernet's work and that undertaken by a group of assistants is most apparent. These collaborators were more draughtsmen than artists and this is reflected in the rather stilted aspect of the images and the way in which outlines have been rather heavily applied to figures and landscapes. In addition, many of the figures are distinguished by an absence of facial expressions and by an unsubtle use of garish colours and hues.

The assistants remain anonymous, although some unsubstantiated sources suggest that Hippolyte Lecomte, Vernet's son-in-law, was among their number. It is more likely that Vernet, unable to accomplish the task on his own, made use of the Depot's own draughtsmen.

Despite the stylistic differences alluded to above, the plates nevertheless offer a fascinating insight into military fashion and the equipment of the imperial armies. The sheer variety of styles, designs and the audacious use of colours – many of which are juxtaposed in a very daring way – still takes one by surprise. The diversity of backgrounds is also rather impressive. Not only is the landscape of France reproduced but we can also spy Italy and Egypt, we can see resplendent mountains or shady forests. Only nocturnal scenes are missing.

NOTE TO READERS

This book, which reproduces plates familiar only to a small group of uniform specialists, does not pretend to be exhaustive or to contain the entire suite of Vernet's images. Nor does it examine the uniforms in any detail or comment upon them – for that the reader is advised to refer to other publications on the subject cited in the bibliography and, in particular, to Jean and Raoul Brunon's *Carle Vernet: La Grande Armée de 1812*, published in 1959, which reproduces twenty-three plates and critically examines each one.

The plates have been selected in an almost random fashion. They provide an impression of the complete work by including a wide variety of plates. The order in which the plates appeared in the original volume has been maintained here, except for that of the officers of Light-Horse which originally appeared between images of dragoons but has now found a more appropriate position.

The images are, of course, not free from human error and contain examples in which the regulations have been misinterpreted or misrepresented. The most frequent mistake was to employ an incorrect colour for an aspect of the uniform. A close reading of the regulatory text and comparison with the images will reveal a number of such infelicities introduced by an artist or by faulty instructions provided to the artist.

It perhaps does not need to be stated that the images should be used with caution and circumspection, and uniform specialists are aware that they need to be used with a certain caution. However, this should not detract from their aesthetic qualities.

Finally, we must return to the question of the Imperial Guard, the most symbolic part of the Napoleonic army. Although they have achieved their reputation through the Napoleonic legend, they must not obscure the rest of Napoleon's troops, who far outnumbered them. Vernet's images are a most precious source on this Grande Armée.

Marshal of the Empire
Full dress uniform

Marshals of the Empire ▶
Undress uniform

Generals in Chief
Full dress uniform

Generals of Division
Undress uniform

14

2nd Regiment of the Guards of Paris
Colonel and *Chef de Bataillon*

2nd Regiment of the Guards of Paris ▶
Grenadiers

Line Infantry
Chef de Bataillon and Colonel

Line Infantry ▶
Officers in overcoats

Light Infantry
Musicians

Line Infantry
Musicians

Line Infantry
Drum Major and Master of Drummers
opposite page

Light Infantry

Line Infantry
Soldiers in waistcoats and fatigue caps

Line Infantry ▶
Grenadiers in waistcoats

Line Infantry
Grenadier *fourriers*
with battalion fanions

Line Infantry ►
Officer and 2nd
Standard-Bearer

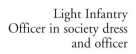

Light Infantry
Officer in society dress
and officer

◄ Line Infantry
Cornet and officer
of voltigeurs

Light Infantry
Officers in greatcoats

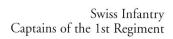

◄ Swiss Infantry
Colonel and superior officer
of the 4th Regiment

Swiss Infantry
2nd Regiment

Swiss Infantry ►
4th Regiment

1st Regiment of Carabiniers
Second Lieutenant in
society dress
Captain in full dress

◄ 1st Regiment of Carabiniers
Colonel in full dress at the
head of his regiment

1st Regiment of Carabiniers
Fourrier
Corporal

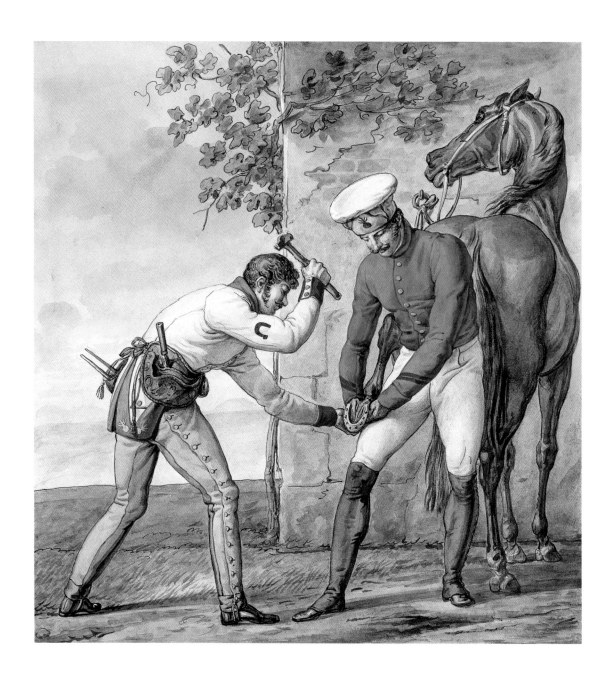

2nd Regiment of Carabiniers ▶
Major in cuirass
Major in society dress

◄ 2nd Regiment of Carabiniers
Squadron Chief

7th Regiment of Cuirassiers
Officers, full service dress, dismounted

10th Regiment of Cuirassiers ▶
Colonel

11th Regiment of Cuirassiers

1st Regiment of Dragoons ▶
Colonel in full dress
Squadron Chief in full dress

◄ 1st Regiment of Dragoons
Colonel

8th Regiment of Dragoons

10th Regiment of Dragoons

16th Regiment of Dragoons
Captain in full dress, mounting his horse
Lieutenant in full dress
opposite page

21st Regiment of Dragoons

23rd Regiment of Dragoons ▶

26th Regiment of Dragoons

◄ 25th Regiment of Dragoons

Heavy cavalry veterinary surgeons

◄ 1st Regiment of Chasseurs à Cheval

7th Regiment of Chasseurs à Cheval

8th Regiment of Chasseurs à Cheval

17th Regiment of Chasseurs à Cheval
opposite page

21st Regiment of Chasseurs à Cheval

22nd Regiment of Chasseurs à Cheval ►
Chasseurs in old-style cloaks

1st Regiment of Hussars

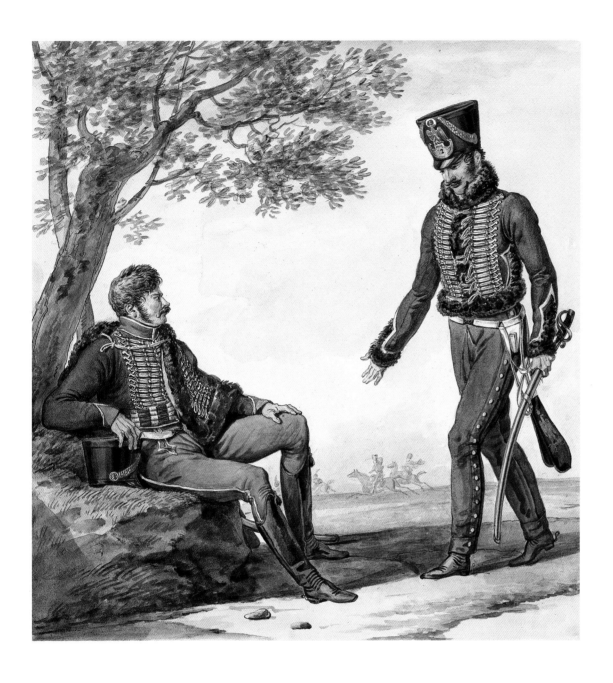

◄ 2nd Regiment of Hussars
Captain in society dress
Major in ball dress

69

◄ 4th Regiment of Hussars

9th Regiment of Hussars
Colonel in full service dress
Squadron Chief in full service dress

10th Regiment of Hussars ▶

5th Regiment of Light-Horse
Colonel and *Chef de Bataillon*

Light-Horse officers in society dress

Light-Horse officers of the ►
1st and 3rd regiments in society dress

3rd Regiment of Light-Horse Lancers

Polish Light-Horse Lancers

8th (Polish) Regiment of Light-Horse Lancers ▶

Artillery
Colonel and *Chef du Bataillon*

Horse Artillery ▶
Colonel

Horse Artillery
Colonel and *Chef du Bataillon*

Horse Artillery ▶
Captain in overalls
Chef du Bataillon in society dress

Horse Artillery
Gunner

Artillery Train
Colonel and *Chef du Bataillon*

Artillery Train ▶
Officers in cloaks

Engineers
Chef du Bataillon and Colonel

Sappers ►

Geographical engineers

BIBLIOGRAPHY

Bucquoy, Eugène-Louis. *Les uniformes du Premier Empire*. Paris, 1977–1985

Chartrand, René. *Napoleonic Wars: Napoleon's Army*. London, 1996

Coppens, Bernard, and Courcelle, Patrice et al. *Les uniformes des guerres napoléoniennes*. Entremont-le-Vieux, 1997–1998. 2 volumes.

Knötel, Herbert, and Elting, Colonel John. *Napoleonic Uniforms*. New York, 1993. 2 volumes.

Lienhart, Doctor, and Humbert, René. *Les uniformes de l'armée française depuis 1690 jusqu'à nos jours*. Leipzig, 1897–1906

Malibran, H. *Guide à l'usage des artistes et des costumiers, contenant la description des uniformes de l'armée française de 1780 à 1848*. Paris, 1907

Rigo (Albert Rigondeau). *Le Plumet. Les uniformes spéciaux et les drapeaux du 1er Empire*. Paris, from 1963. A series of plates.

Rousselot, Lucien. *L'armée française. Ses uniformes. Son armement. Son équipement*. Paris, 1943–1971

Vernet, Horace. *Collection des uniformes des armées françaises de 1791 à 1824*. Paris, 1822–1825. 2 volumes.

Printed by
Artegrafica S.p.A.
Verona